A piebald cob at the show 'Edward'

Welsh mountain ponies relax in the field 'Foxwoods Hoity-Toity' and 'Winneydene Sunrise'

'Lilly', daughter of Dartmoor pony 'Kayben Felicity'

Welsh mountain pony 'Escley Triumph'

Trakehner mare 'Muschamp Issabella'

Trakehner mare 'Muschamp Issabella'

Thoroughbred gelding 'Sur La Mer'

New Forest pony 'Woottonheath Tom Tom'

Companions for life

Exmoor Pony by 'Tarquin'

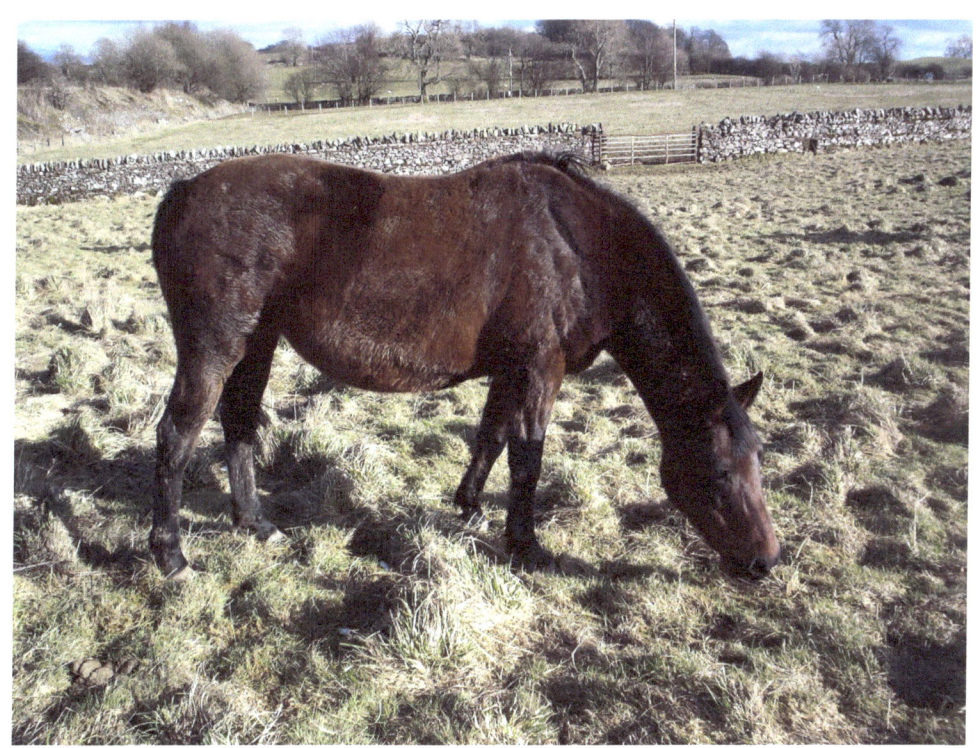

Show hunter 'Foxwood Damson'

Shetland pony 'Lladyl Palimpsest'

Willacy's Salvador and Gilfach Zani

'Lantyan High Society' with companion foal 'Rowhill Midnight'

Foal 'Foxwood Thorn'

Appaloosa youngsters 'Cock-o-the-Walk' and 'Cappuccino Jack'

Fell pony 'Wansfell Teasel'

A very young foal

Curiosity

New Forest pony 'Rowhill Midnight'

Shetland champion 'Lladyl Palimpsest'

New Forest pony 'Woottonheath Tom Tom'

New Forest ponies 'Rowhill Midnight' and 'Woottonheath Tom Tom'